HOT SONGS MICHAEL BOLTON

Production: Stephen Clark
and Sadie Cook
First Published 1994

IMP

Southend Road, Woodford Green, Essex IG8 8HN, England

HOW AM I SUPPOSED TO LIVE WITHOUT YOU

Words and Music by
MICHAEL BOLTON and DOUG JAMES

Bb/F F/Eb Bb/D F/C Bb
They said you were leav - in', some-one's
And how can I blame you when I
F/A Eb/G Ebm/Gb Bb/F
swept your heart a - way. From the look up - on your face, I see it's
build my world a - round the hope that one day we'd be so much more than
C/E Fsus4 F/Eb Dm7 Bb/D
true. So tell me all a - bout it, tell me 'bout the plans you're mak -
friends. Now, I don't wan - na know the price I'm gon - na pay for dream-
Ebmaj7 Bb/D Cm7 Gm7 Dm7 Eb Fsus4 F7
in', tell me one thing more be - fore I go.
ing, ev - en now it's more than I can take.
Tell me

Ebmaj7 F/Eb Dm7 Gm7 Ebmaj7 F/Eb
3fr.
how am I _ sup - posed _ to live _ with - out _ you,
now that I've been lov - in' you _ so
f
Dm7 Bb7sus4 Bb7 Ebmaj7 F/Eb Dm7 Gm7
long. _
How am I _ sup - posed _ to live _ with - out _ you
and
Cm7 Bb/D Ebmaj7 Fsus4 F/G Gm7 Cm7 Bb/D Ebmaj7 Fsus4
how am I _ sup - posed _ to car - ry on _
when all that I've _ been liv - in' for _ is
1. Ebmaj7 F/Eb Dm7 D7-9
4fr.
gone.
mp
2. Bb Bb/D
gone.

E♭ Fsus4 Gm7 F/A B/F♯ F♯ F♯/E
3fr.
Now,
D♯m7 B/D♯ Emaj7 B/D♯
6fr.
I don't wan-na know the price_ I'm gon-na pay_ for dream - ing,
C♯m7 G♯m7 B/D♯ C♯m7 F♯sus4 E/F♯ D♯m7
4fr. 4fr. 4fr. 6fr.
now that your_ dream has come true.
Tell me
Emaj7 F♯/E D♯m7 G♯m7 Emaj7 F♯/E
6fr. 4fr.
how am I_ sup-posed_ to live_ with-out_ you
now that I've been lov - in' you_ so

D♯m7
6fr.
B7sus4
2fr.
B7
Emaj7
F♯/E
long.
How am I supposed to live without
D♯m7
6fr.
G♯m7
4fr.
C♯m7
4fr.
B/D♯
x0
Emaj7
out you
and how am I supposed to carry on
F♯sus4
F♯/G♯
x
G♯m7
4fr.
C♯m7
4fr.
B/D♯
x0
Emaj7
F♯sus4
when all that I've been livin' for is
Emaj7
F♯/E
D♯m7+5
x
6fr.
C♯m7
4fr.
B(addC♯)
x
4fr.
gone.
mp
rit.

KNOCK ON WOOD

Words and Music by
EDDIE FLOYD and STEPHEN CROPPER

sure - ly, Sure - ly lose a lot 'Cause your love
ba - by. Ba - by, I'm in a trance. 'Cause your love
it that I set e - nough. Just one touch
A7
is bet - ter than an - y love I know.
is bet - ter than an - y love I know.
is bet - ter, you know it means so much.
E7
A7
It's like thun - der, light - ning,
E7
A7
E7
the way you love me is frighten - ing. Think I bet - ter knock on wood,

To Coda
E5
G5
3 fr
A5
B5
D5
5 fr
ba - by I bet - ter knock.
1.
B5
I'm not sup - er -
2.
B5
A5
G5
3 fr
F♯
G♯
4 fr
A
C
B7
D.S. al Coda
Ain't no
Repeat and fade
Coda
B5
A5
G5
3 fr
E7
A7
Think I bet - ter knock, (knock) knock, (knock) knock on wood. _ Bet - ter

LEAN ON ME

Words and Music by
BILL WITHERS

F Gm 3fr F
C7 Dm C
F
Lean on me,
F
Gm 3fr Am B♭
Am Gm 3fr F
Gm 3fr Am
when you're not strong, and I'll be your friend, I'll help you car -
Gm 3fr B♭/C F
Gm 3fr Am B♭
Am Gm 3fr F
- ry on, for it won't be long, till I'm gon - na need
C7 B♭ C7
F
F
Gm 3fr Am B♭
somebody to lean on. Please swal-low your pride,

Am Gm F Gm Am Gm B♭/C
— if I have things — you need to bor - row, —
F Gm Am B♭ Am Gm F
for — no one can fill — those of your needs —
C7 B♭ C7 F
— that you won't let — show. — You can just
F
call on me bro - ther, when you need a hand, we all need some-bo - dy to lean —

on. I just might have a prob - lem that you'll un - der - stand, we all
C G7 C7 F
need some - bo - dy to lean on. Lean on
Gm Am B♭ Am Gm F Gm Am
me, when you're not strong, and I'll be your friend, I'll help you car -
If there is a load, you have to bear that you can't car -
Gm B♭/C F Gm Am B♭ Am Gm F
- ry on, for it won't be long, till I'm gon - na need
- ry, I'm right up the road, I'll share your load

C7
B♭
C7
1.
F
2.
F
somebody to lean on. You can just me.
if you just call
Gm/F
F
3fr
Call me, call me, call me,
1.
2.
a tempo
C11
call me. call me.
B♭
Lean on

F
B♭
F
Gm
3fr
Am
me, when you're not strong, I'll be your friend, I'll help you car -
B♭
F
B♭/F
3
B♭
- ry on, for it won't be long, till I'm gon-na
3
F
C7
F
F
need some-bo - dy, some-bo-dy to lean on. Lean on,
B♭7
F
B♭7
repeat ad lib. to fade
lean on me, lean on, lean on me.

LOVE IS A WONDERFUL THING

Words and Music by
MICHAEL BOLTON and ANDY GOLDMARK

Moderate Rhythm and Blues

No chord
Birds fly, they don't think twice,_ they simp-ly spread their wings.__
The on-ly thing a riv - er knows_ is run-nin' to the sea.___
The sun shines, it don't ask why,_
And ev - ery spring when a flow - er grows,_
G/D
D
or what the whole thing means.__
it hap-pens nat - ural - ly.___
The same ap-plies to
The same mag - ic when you're
G/D
D
G/D
D
you and I, we nev - er ques - tion that.___
in my arms, no log - ic can de - fine.___

G
Bm
Asus4
So good; it's just un-der - stood._
Ain't no con-jec-ture, just a
Don't know why, just feels so right._
I on-ly know it hap-pens
A
D
Bm7
mat-ter of fact._
ev-er-y time._
Love_ is a won-der-ful thing,_
A
D/F♯
G
D
Bm7
make you smile_ through the pour-ing rain._
Love_ is a won-der-ful thing,_
Em7
Em7/A
I'll say it a-gain_ and a-gain._

D
A/B
Bm7
E7/G♯
G
Turn your world in - to one sweet dream, take your heart and make
D/F♯
Em7
Em7/A
it sing. Love, (love,) love, is a won - der - ful
1.
D
G/D
D
G/D
D
G/D
D
thing.
G/D
D
2.
D
G/D
D
G/D
D
thing.

F♯m7
Bm7
A/B
Oh, when the cold wind blows, I know you're gon - na
Bm7
A/B
Bm7
Em7
F♯m7
be there to warm me. Oh, that's what keeps me go - in', and
Gmaj9
3fr.
Gmaj9/A
our sweet love will keep on grow - in', just keeps grow - in'.
D
G/D
D
G/D
D
G/D
D
G/D
D

F
G
Am7/D
D
Am7/D
D
F
G
Em7/A
A
E♭
Cm7
Love is a
B♭
E♭/G
A♭
won - der - ful thing,
make you smile through the pour - ing rain.
Love

Eb
Cm7
3fr.
Fm7
Fm7/Bb
— is a won-der-ful thing, —
I'll say it a-gain —
Eb
Bb/C
Cm7
3fr.
— and a-gain. —
Turn your world in-to one sweet dream, —
F7/A
Ab
4fr.
Eb/G
Ab
4fr.
take your heart — and — make — it sing. —
Love, — (love,) — love, —
Eb/G
Ab
4fr.
— is a won-der-ful ... love, — (love,) —
love is a won-der-ful ...

Eb/G
Cm7
3fr.
Fm7
Fm7/Bb
N.C.
love, (love, love,) love is a won-der-ful... (Spoken): thing.
Fm7/Bb
Repeat and fade (vocal ad lib)
Eb
Ab/Eb
4fr.
Eb
Ab/Eb
4fr.
Eb
Love is a won - der-ful, won-der-ful thing.
Ab/Eb
4fr.
Eb
Ab/Eb
4fr.
Eb
Ab/Eb
4fr.
Eb
Love is a won - der-ful, won-der-ful thing. Love is a won - der-ful,
Ab/Eb
4fr.
Eb
Ab/Eb
4fr.
Eb
Ab/Eb
4fr.
Eb
won-der-ful thing. Love is a won - der-ful, won-der-ful thing.

THE ONE THING

Words and Music by
MICHAEL BOLTON, DIANE WARREN and DESMOND CHILD

Bb/D
Cm7
4fr
Abadd9
the one thing.
the one thing.
Eb
Bb/D
Cm7
4fr
Peo-ple come and peo-ple go, the way the winds of
Time-less as the stars, faith-ful as the sea, like the end-less ris-ing sun, I know you'll be
Abadd9
Eb
Bb/D
for - tune blow, so hard to find that heart of gold, I re -
there for me. There's so much love in - side me, this heart of mine could break, 'cause I
Cm7
4fr
Abadd9
- mem - ber some - one told me, when you find it, don't let go. You're the
know I've found for - ev - er, and with ev - ery breath I take.

Chorus
E♭
Gm7
A♭add 9
one thing, you're the one thing ba - by, makes this world hea - ven,
B♭11
E♭
Gm7
makes the whole thing right. You're the one thing that means some - thing ba - by, the
Cm7
4fr
Gm/B♭
A♭maj7
B♭11
one I be - lieve in, the one thing I need in my
1.
A♭add 9
life.
2.
A♭11
life.

D♭maj7
And your love is like a rain - bow
Fm7
in a world that's black and white,
G♭
paint my dreams in
col - our,
A♭11
and your arms be-come a - live.
A♭
D♭maj7
You're my ev-ery in-spi - ra - tion,
Fm7
you're the wings that make me fly

Bbm
Bbm/Ab
Gb
you're my on - ly des - ti - na - tion, you're the one thing, the one thing in my
life.
Eb
Bb/D
Cm7
4fr
Abadd9
Eb
The one
Bb/D
Cm7
4fr
Abadd9
D.𝄋
Chorus ad lib. to fade
thing.
You're the

REACH OUT, I'LL BE THERE

Words and Music by
BRIAN HOLLAND, LAMONT DOZIER and EDDIE HOLLAND

Abm7
4fr
Db
4fr
feel that you can't go on 'cause all
lost and a - bout to give up 'cause your best
tell the way you hang your head, you're with - out
of your hope is gone, and your life
just ain't good e - nough, and you feel
love and now you're a - fraid and through your
is filled with much con - fu - sion un - til hap -
the world has grown cold and you're drift -
tears you look a - round, but there's no
pi - ness is just an il - lu - sion, and your world
ing out all on your own, and you need
peace of mind to be found. (I know what you're thinking,

Abm7
Db
— a-round is crum-bling down. — Well dar - ling, —
— a hand to hold. — Dar - ling, —
you're alone in the world, no love of your own.) But dar - ling, —
Gb/Bb
Gb
reach out, — dar - ling,
reach out, — (Come on girl, reach on out for me) dar - ling,
reach out, — (Come on girl, reach on out for me) dar - ling,
Bb/D
F°7
reach out — for me. —
reach out — for me. —
reach out — for me. —
1st time only
No Chord
N.C.
Bb
I'll be there, —
I'll be there, —
I'll be there, —

Eb/Bb
Ebm
Bb
to give you all the love you need. And
with a love that will shel-ter you. And
to give you all the love you need. And
Eb/Bb
Ebm
I'll be there, you can al - ways count on me.
I'll be there, with a love that will see you through.
I'll be there, you can al - ways count on me.
1.
Bb
When you feel
2.
Bb
Eb/Bb
Ebm
I'll be there, to give you all the love you need.
I'll be there, with a love that will shel-ter you.

Bb
Eb/Bb
And I'll be there, you can
I'll be there, with a
Ebm
To Coda
Bb
D.S. (no repeat) al Coda
al - ways count on me.
love to see you through.
I can
Coda
Bb
Repeat and fade
Bb
I'll be there.
Eb/Bb
Ebm
6fr
Bb

SAID I LOVED YOU, BUT I LIED

Words and Music by
MICHAEL BOLTON and ROBERT JOHN 'MUTT' LANGE

E♭ 6fr
B♭
till the end of time.
I've found it in you.
You came to me like the dawn
So ma-ny rea-sons in so
Cm 3fr
A♭ 4fr
B♭
B♭sus4
B♭
through the night, just shin - ing like the sun,
ma-ny ways, my life has just be-gun,
Cm 3fr
A♭ 4fr
B♭
out of my dreams and in-to my life, you are the one, you are
need you for ev - er, but I need you to say: you are the one, you are
E♭ 6fr
B♭
Cm 3fr
A♭add 9 4fr
the one.
the one.
Said I loved you but I

E♭
6fr
B♭
Cm
3fr
A♭add 9
4fr
lied, 'cause this is more than love I
E♭
6fr
B♭
Cm
3fr
A♭add 9
4fr
feel in - side, said I loved you but I was
E♭
6fr
B♭
Cm
3fr
A♭add 9
4fr
wrong, 'cause love can ne - ver ev - er
E♭
6fr
B♭
Cm
3fr
Gm
3fr
feel so strong, said I loved you but I lied.

1.
2.
D
D
Guitar solo
E♭m
C♭
D♭
G♭
C♭
B♭
E♭m
C♭
D♭
G♭
C♭
B♭
Cm
A♭
You came to me like the dawn__ through the night,__ just shin -

B♭
B♭sus4
B♭
3fr
-ing like the sun.
Out of my dreams and in-
A♭
4fr
B♭sus4
-to my life, you are the one, you are the one.
F
C
Dm
B♭
I said I loved you but I lied,
F
C
Dm
B♭
F
C
'cause this is more than love I feel in-side.
Said I loved you but I was

Dm
B♭
F
C
Dm
B♭
wrong, 'cause love can ne - ver ev - er feel so strong.
F
C
Dm
Am
I said I loved you 'cause this is more than love I feel in - side.
E
Am
I said I loved you but I lied.
repeat to fade

WHEN A MAN LOVES A WOMAN

Words and Music by
CALVIN LEWIS and ANDREW WRIGHT

Ab/C Bbm7 Db/Ab Gb 1.Gb/Ab
4fr.
see it. She can do no wrong Turn his back on his best friend if he
com - forts, and sleep out in the rain, if she said that's the
Db Gb/Ab 2.Gb/Ab Db Db9 Gb
puts her down. When a way it ought to be. When a
Db Db9 Gb Db
man loves a wom-an, I give you ev - ery - thing I've got.
Db9 Gb Db Ab/C Bbm7 Eb
Try - ing to hold on to your pre - cious love. Ba - by, ba - by,

Eb7
Ebm7/Ab
11fr.
N.C.
D
please don't treat me bad.
When a man loves a
A/C#
Bm7
D/A
G
wom - an, deep down in his soul, she can
G/A
3fr.
D
G/A
3fr.
D
bring him such mis - e - ry.
If she is play - ing him for a
A/C#
Bm7
D/A
G
fool, he's the last one to know.
Lov - ing

G/A D G/A D
eyes can nev - er see. Yes, when a man loves a
A/C♯ Bm7 D/A G
freely
wom-an, I know ex - act - ly how he feels, 'cause
G/A
ba - by, ba - by... When a
Repeat and fade
D A/C♯ Bm7 G/A
man loves a wom - an. When a

SOUL OF MY SOUL

Words and Music by
MICHAEL BOLTON, DIANE WARREN and WALTER AFANASIEFF

F♯m7
B7sus4
2fr
E
B/D♯
things we just don't un - der - stand.
So blind to each oth - er, we on - ly
all I ev - er want for you.
The love you be - lieve in, your ev - ery
A/C♯
C6
F♯m7
see one side of no - where,
some things we may
dream, your ev - ery pas - sion,
in time I know you'll
E/G♯
Aadd 9
B7sus4
2fr
ne - ver know,
if there's one thing you should ev - er know.
come to see,
no - thing means as much to me.

D♭
4fr
G♭maj7
B♭m7
6fr
Soul of my soul, heart of my heart. the great-est treas-ure of my
Soul of my soul, heart of my heart, some kind of mi - ra - cle of
E♭m7
A♭7sus4
4fr
D♭
4fr
G♭maj7
life, that's what you are. Soul of my soul, child of my heart,
life, that's what you are.
E♭m7
A♭7sus4
4fr
B♭♭dim5add 9
5fr
1.
D♭
4fr
I love you more than you know, soul of my soul.
2.
F♯m
A/E
B/D♯
soul. There'll come a time when you'll be on your own,

A/C♯
B/C♯
C♯m
4fr
F♯m7
but in your heart you're ne - ver far from home.
Ev - ery road you take, your ev -
E/G♯
A
B11
2fr
Guitar solo
- ery liv - ing day, you will al - ways be, you will al - ways be.
C
Fmaj9
3fr
Am7
Dm7
G11
3fr
3
C
Am7
Dm7
G11
3fr
G

Reproduced and printed by
Halstan & Co. Ltd., Amersham, Bucks., England

ABRSM PUBLISHING

The Associated Board of the Royal Schools of Music

Theory of Music Examinations

GRADE 6

1999